cover cover

Bible Study

7 Sessions for Home and Personal Use

Rivers
of
Justice

Responding to God's call
to righteousness today

Ruth Valerio

Contents

Introduction

The title for this *Cover to Cover* Bible study, *Rivers of Justice*, comes from an Old Testament passage: Amos 5:24. Then in Micah 6:8 the question is asked, 'What does the LORD require of you?'; so we ask ourselves: how should we respond? Amos and Micah were contemporaries, speaking during the eighth century BC after the nation of Israel had split into two kingdoms (this happened after the reign of Solomon). Amos speaks to the northern kingdom of Israel and Micah to the southern kingdom of Judah. On the surface this was a good period of peace and prosperity. Yet the reality under the surface was rotten, with social and moral corruption rife. The two prophets have many words of judgment to speak, but into the whirlwind of their prophecies come these two beautiful verses.

Both prophets speak about the sort of worship that God does and does not want His people to offer to Him (Amos 5:21–24; Micah 6:6–8). Amos describes a situation where the poor are trampled and the righteous are oppressed (5:11–12), but he cries out, 'let justice roll on like a river, righteousness like a never-failing stream!' It is a stunning picture of the dramatic effect that justice and righteousness can have, sweeping inexorably through the dirt and the sorrow, bringing cleansing, healing and joy. Micah then asks what the people can do that will please God: how are they to respond to the accusations of their sinfulness? He replies that they are 'to act justly and to love mercy and to walk humbly with [their] God'. Here we see one of the best descriptions of true worship as Micah brings his words down to a fully personal level.

The question for us is: what relevance do these words bear now? To put it at its simplest, the Bible is the story of God's dealings with His creation. It tells how He made the universe, the world and everything that lives in it, but how the humans He put in charge of looking after that world rebelled against Him and went away from the calling He had given them (we shall look at this further in our studies together). The rest of the Bible story then focuses on how God sets about putting this situation back to rights again; in other words, His plans for salvation ('salvation history'). This happens first through the calling of Israel and then ultimately in the life, death and resurrection of Jesus, leading to the missionary task given to His disciples (again, we shall look more fully later on at what that 'missionary task' entailed). The Bible story finishes with a look into the future, giving us glimpses of what the end of the story looks like (which is, of course, really just the beginning!). As followers of Jesus, our role is to live the story of the Bible in our own lives.

As we shall see, when we get to know this story, what we find is that it has justice at its heart. The well-known American speaker and social activist, Jim Wallis, tells the story of his friend who cut out of his Bible all references to the poor or to poverty. When he had finished he did not have much of a Bible left and Jim Wallis used to borrow that Bible when he spoke in churches and ask people whether they had 'a holy Bible that was full of holes'. The point is well made! In our churches and in our own spiritual lives, we can focus on many things: our worship, our prayer life, our evangelism, our fellowship together, living holy lives and so on. All of these are important and right, but it is also good to ask ourselves whether we are as full of holes as that Bible.

The hope for this Bible study is that it will begin to fill in some of those holes. Our seven weeks together will focus on two things. Firstly, we will learn more about that story that is told through the Bible and we will discover more how the strong thread of justice weaves its way through the narrative. So, quite simply, we are going to take a week each to look at what is said about justice in the Old Testament, in the life of Jesus, and through the example and writing of the earliest Church (ie, the New Testament outside of the Gospels). In our fourth week together we will explore more fully our role as carers of God's earth as this is perhaps one of the biggest holes in our churches!

Then, secondly, we will look at some key issues we face today if we want to play our part in letting justice 'roll on like a river'. Week 5 will look at the hugely important issues of global trade and debt; Week 6 will tackle the thorny questions surrounding money and then, finally, Week 7 will look at the challenges of living in a consumer-driven society. Through all this we will ask the practical question of Micah: what does the Lord require of me?[1]

The challenges these weeks will present us with may often be tough and we will need to be prepared to lower our defences and be honest with one another. However, as we face these things together we can be excited with the prospect, not only of learning how rivers of justice roll through the Bible, but of how we can keep them rolling through our lives, through our churches and out into the wider world.

---

[1] To look at all of this in more depth than we are able to do here, see R. Valerio, *L is for Lifestyle: Christian living that doesn't cost the earth* (IVP, 2004).

WEEK 1

Rivers of Justice in the Old Testament

Opening Icebreaker

Spend time introducing yourselves to one another, if necessary, and having a drink. Make people feel relaxed and comfortable. Then pair up with someone you don't know well. Find out two things about your partner (as serious or as funny as you like) and then introduce each other back into the wider group.

Bible Readings

- Genesis 9:1–7
- Deuteronomy 24:10–22
- Psalm 146
- Proverbs 29:7
- Isaiah 58:1–14

Opening Our Eyes

The more awake amongst us may have noticed that the readings for this week's Bible study span the various stages of the history that is recounted in the Old Testament. Genesis 9:1–7 comes from what is called the 'pre-history' narrative of Genesis chapters 1–11, before the story of Israel begins with the calling of Abram in Genesis 12. The book of Deuteronomy is placed as Israel stands at the threshold of entering into the land that Yahweh had promised them. Moses delivers one final address to the people. He reminds them of what has happened to them since Yahweh rescued them from Egypt (chaps 1–3), before teaching them many laws from Yahweh so that they will be able to live successfully in their new land (chaps 4–29); 24:10–22 is set in this context. Psalm 146 and Proverbs 19:7 come from different times during the reign of the kings over Israel and, depending on your view of the authorship of Isaiah, Isaiah 58 may come from the time when Israel had returned from exile in Babylon.

As we saw in the Introduction to this study guide, the Bible tells the story of God's plans for salvation for what He has made. After nearly wiping out the whole of His creation through the Flood, God, in a sense, starts again and calls Abram to be the founder of the nation of Israel (Gen. 12:1–3). This nation always had a purpose: to be a blessing to the other nations and hence be the means through which all peoples would be brought into a full relationship with the one God, Yahweh (see also Exod. 19:6 and Isa. 42:5–7; 49:6).

Thus, foundationally, Israel was called to serve and to exist for the sake of the other nations. The significance of this was that they were then called to live in such a way as would show the other peoples who this God, Yahweh, was and what He was like, and so be the means by which the nations would be attracted to Him.

The laws that set the pattern for how Israel was to live are laid out from Exodus 19 through Leviticus, Numbers and Deuteronomy (with narrative episodes in between). All these laws are based on one thing: the Exodus. This was Yahweh's deliverance of the people from the bondage that they faced in Egypt (see the Deuteronomy reading above) and, to put it at its simplest, Israel was called to demonstrate a way of living that was radically alternative to the regime they had been under in Egypt. Hence they were to reject any form of oppression and live lives that showed compassion and care for those who were needy.

Sadly, of course, Israel failed all too often (just read the history of the kings!). Instead of seeing their position as one of service, they thought they had been chosen by God to assume a position of privilege and elitism. By doing so, Israel became just like the other nations around – full of nationalism and pride. And so they forgot their call to justice, which was such a central part of how they were to be a beacon in the midst of the other peoples.

The books of the Old Testament are many and varied, but through them all we see God's call to His people to live in a way that would bring others to Him.

Discussion Starters

1. Proverbs 29:7 is very blunt in its description of one of the characteristics of someone who is righteous. Is this how you would have described the word 'righteous'? What do you think is the relationship between justice and righteousness?

_____

_____

_____

_____

_____

2. Genesis 9:1–7 gives one of the founding principles as to why we should care for other people. What is that principle and why is it so important?

_____

_____

_____

_____

_____

3. Why, according to Deuteronomy 24, were the Israelites to demonstrate compassion for those who were needy? Try to explain in your own words why that was so significant.

_____

_____

_____

_____

_____

4. What are some things that God has done for you in your life that He asks you, therefore, to do for others?

_____

_____

_____

_____

5. Look at each of the commands in Deuteronomy 24:10–22 and discuss how these might be relevant today.

_____

_____

_____

_____

_____

6. If someone asked you to describe God, what words would you use? Compare these with the description in Psalm 146.

_____

_____

_____

_____

_____

7. The people of Isaiah's day complained that God did not come close to them. Why didn't He (Isa. 58:3–5)? What does Yahweh want His people to do instead?

_____

_____

_____

_____

_____

8. What have you learnt from today's study for your church and for your own life?

_____

_____

_____

_____

Personal Application

As we saw in the Introduction, the words of the Old Testament are not just relevant for those for whom they were first written or spoken. Down through the centuries they speak to us still. In our Bible readings today we have seen how God is a God who has justice at the heart of who He is and what He does. He called a people, Israel, to demonstrate this and hence be the means by which other peoples came to Him. Significantly, one of the key verses that talks about this (Exod. 19:6) is, in 1 Peter 2:9 (and see further, vv.10–12), used of the Church. The calling, therefore, is given to us too. We are to live lives that show that we worship a God who loves justice.

Seeing Jesus in the Scriptures

We will, of course, look at this more fully next week, so not much needs to be said here. However, it is good to remember now that God's story that we find in the Old Testament is pointing towards, and finds its fulfilment in, Jesus and what He does for us through His life, death and resurrection (see Luke 24:25–27). It is through Jesus, as He brings about the New Exodus through being the Passover Lamb (John 1:29), that we are enabled to become the people of God. He is the true Image of God (Col. 1:15) and we ultimately come to know about God and worship God fully only through Him (John 14:6–7).

WEEK 2

Rivers of Justice in Jesus

Opening Icebreaker

Tell each other what has been the best part and the worst part of the past week, since you last met as a group.

Bible Readings

- Matthew 11:1–5; 25:31–46
- Luke 1:46–55; 4:16–21; 10:25–37
- Revelation 21:1–22:7 (you can skip 21:12–22 if need be)

 **Opening Our Eyes**

As we have seen, Israel was called to be the means through which the nations would come to worship Yahweh. Yet Israel failed in this dismally and paid for it by seeing her land ruined and her top people sent into exile in Babylon. By the time of the New Testament, Israel was back in her own land (see Ezra and Nehemiah), but was under the rule of Rome. Instead of serving the nations through being a blessing to them, Israel was forced into servitude by an oppressive regime.

There were different views as to how to respond to Roman rule. Some – the Zealots – argued for violent uprising and rebellion. Others – the aristocratic Sadduccees – secured their own political advantage by working to please the Romans. A third group – the Pharisees – were the religious purists who demanded that the Law be kept down to its smallest detail, and a final group – the Essenes – were a sect that removed themselves totally and lived in the desert near the Dead Sea.

Into this situation came Jesus, with a message of His own: 'Repent, for the kingdom of heaven is at hand' (Matt. 4:17, NKJV). All of the above groups assumed that the Jews were the chosen people of God, superior to the Romans. Only Jesus challenged their racial elitism and preached and demonstrated good news that was to reach beyond the Jews to the Gentiles (Matt. 28:19; Luke 13:29–30). The good news was that – through His life, death and resurrection – Jesus was opening the way for people to be reconciled to God (2 Cor. 5:14–21) and so for the whole world to be brought back in line with God's good purposes (v.19 and also John 3:16–17; Rom. 8:19–21). As Israel was called to demonstrate justice and compassion, so Jesus exemplified this in His own life, welcoming those whom the Jews traditionally excluded from God's kingdom (eg Mark 1:40ff; 5:21ff; John 4:1ff).

The really exciting part, according to Jesus, was that this was to start now – not at some future moment in time when everyone had died, but NOW! During a debate as to how He could cast out demons, Jesus stated, 'If I drive out demons by the finger of God, then the kingdom of God has come to you' (Luke 11:20). Because of Jesus' presence on earth as a human being (a part of God's creation), because He took humanity's sins on Himself on a cross, because God raised Him from the dead, because of all these things, God's plans for the world begin to become reality in the present.

And yet not all the Gospel accounts of Jesus' life finish with Him here on earth and, having appeared to many people after His resurrection, Jesus goes 'up' into heaven (Luke 24:50–51; John implies this in his Gospel, 21:22, and Mark 16:9–20, though almost certainly not original to Mark, does show that the Ascension was well known by the time it was added). God's plans have not yet come to fruition fully. We know that Jesus has triumphed over the evil that thwarts God's purposes and so we see glimpses of those purposes now (the Holy Spirit is our guarantee of this: Eph. 1:13–14). Yet we also know that we will not see these things completely until Jesus comes again. As Jesus' followers, we are in strange times; called to live as children of the future, anticipating that future in the way we live our lives today.

Discussion Starters

1. Try to say in a sentence what Jesus came to this earth to do.

_____

_____

_____

2. Luke 1:46–55 is an example of what has been called 'the upside-down kingdom'. In what ways was the kingdom that Jesus talked about 'upside-down' to what the Jews were expecting?

_____

_____

_____

3. Discuss some of the ways in which the Isaiah 61 passage Jesus read out in the synagogue was fulfilled by Him (Luke 4:21).

_____

_____

_____

4. The story of the sheep and the goats (Matt. 25:31–46) talks about our responsibility to fellow disciples of Jesus who are hungry, thirsty, naked or in prison (see Leader's Notes for a fuller explanation of this). How do we apply that today?

_____

_____

_____

5. In what ways does Jesus show a concern for physical and social – as well as spiritual – needs? For starters, you can look at Matthew 4:23; 9:33.

_____

_____

6. Looking at the parable of the Good Samaritan (Luke 10:25–37), contrast the attitudes and behaviour of the priest, the Levite and the Samaritan. Why do you think each one does what he does?

_____

_____

_____

7. In Luke 10:29 the expert in the Law asks Jesus, 'who is my neighbour?', but Jesus seems to turn that question around in His answer and says, in effect, '_You_ are the neighbour, so go and do likewise' (vv.36–37)! In what ways and to whom is God asking you to be a 'neighbour' today?

_____

_____

_____

8. Revelation 21–22 gives us, in pictorial language, a description of what the future is going to be like when Jesus has come back to earth and when both heaven and earth are renewed. What will be some of the characteristics of that future?

_____

_____

_____

9. As we pray, 'Your kingdom come, your will be done on earth as it is in heaven' (Matt. 6:10), so we are to work to see that partly happening now. How does that shape the way we live our lives and determine the things we should make a priority?

_____

_____

_____

Personal Application

Jesus lived an extraordinary life and did many amazing things. Whilst not everything He did is for us to copy (eg His baptism in the River Jordan and, obviously, His crucifixion), He is the supreme model for our lives (eg 1 Cor. 11:1; Phil. 2:5; 1 Pet. 2:21). He sets us a standard when we look at how He reached out to those who were excluded by society and showed compassion for social, spiritual and physical needs all together. Think of how you, too, can reach out beyond your immediate family and circle of friends, to love those whom God has created and for whom Jesus died.

Seeing Jesus in the Scriptures

Jesus came full of contradictions. The King of kings, yet He was born in a stable to a poor teenage girl. A revolutionary, yet He preached against living by the sword (Matt. 26:52). He spoke of a righteousness that was to surpass that practised by the religious leaders (Matt. 5:20), but spent time with those considered most unrighteous. Through His life and death He brought in an 'upside-down kingdom' that turned on its head all the expectations of the day. Let us follow the examples of Mary and of Zechariah in praising the God of Israel, 'because he has come and has redeemed his people' (Luke 1:68).

WEEK 3

Rivers of Justice in the Early Church

Opening Icebreaker

Share how long you have been a part of your local church and why you enjoy it.

Bible Readings

- Acts 2:42–47; 4:32–35
- James 1:26–2:26

Opening Our Eyes

Last week we looked at Jesus and how, in fulfilling the calling of Israel, He is the model for our engagement with justice issues. He had compassion on those who were around Him. He radically included those who were unloved and were pushed to the margins of society. In His death He ultimately opened the way for people to be brought back from exile, into God's kingdom.

At the time, though, His death left people devastated and bewildered: how could He be the Messiah and yet die a failure at the hands of the Romans (Luke 24:19–21)? The answer lay in a true understanding of His death. On the cross, Jesus took on Himself all the sins of humanity (as did, metaphorically, the scapegoat in Leviticus 16): the personal sins of individual people and all the evils they create. That was not the end though, of course, because God then raised Jesus from the dead and gave Him new resurrection life. In doing this, victory was proclaimed over death; over the evil spiritual forces and over all the sin, injustices and suffering that accompany them.

The story we have been following so far does not stop there, however, and Luke makes it clear that his second book (Acts) is all about what Jesus continued 'to do and to teach' after He was taken up to heaven (Acts 1:1–2). Jesus carries on what He started when on earth; but now He continues that through His followers, who are equipped to do that through the ministry/work of His Holy Spirit (Acts 1:4–8).

The Bishop of Durham, Tom Wright, has famously described the biblical story as like a play with five acts: Creation, the Fall, Israel, Jesus and then the fifth act which is the Church. The script in this final act breaks off though at an early point, so that there is a large gap between the beginning of Act Five and its final ending (ie the return of Jesus and the new heavens and earth). We are like actors, given the task of so immersing ourselves in the play as we have it that we are then able to continue it on in our own lives as we think would be consistent with what we have seen so far of the script, the characters and, especially, the author.

Thankfully we are able to see the beginning of Act Five and get an idea of what the Church should look like. Listen to this description of the Church from an Early Church historian called Aristides:

> They walk in all humility and kindness, and falsehood is not found among them, and they love one another. They don't despise the widow and don't upset the orphan. He who has gives liberally to he who has not. If they see a stranger, they bring him under their roof and rejoice over him, as it were their own brother … and if they hear that any of their number is imprisoned or oppressed for the name of their Messiah, all of them provide for his needs, and if it is possible that they may be delivered, they deliver him. And if there is among them a person who is poor and needy, and they have not an abundance of necessaries, they fast two or three days that they may supply the needy with their necessary food.

Wouldn't it be wonderful if a contemporary church historian could write the same about your church?!

Discussion Starters

1. The descriptions of the earliest Church in Acts 2:42–47 comes straight after Pentecost, and that in Acts 4:32–35 immediately after the believers were all filled with the Holy Spirit (v.31). Is this how you would have described a church that was 'full of the Holy Spirit'? In what ways might your description have differed?

_____

_____

_____

_____

_____

2. Are there any things that particularly strike you about these descriptions?

_____

_____

_____

_____

_____

3. Go through and jot down all the characteristics of the Early Church in these Acts passages. In what ways are they relevant to your church?

_____

_____

_____

_____

_____

4. Look at James' description of a religion that is pure and faultless and hence acceptable to God (1:27). What do you think his description means?

_____

_____

_____

_____

5. Can you think of examples of where churches today show favouritism towards people with more money than others?

_____

_____

_____

_____

_____

6. How would you explain the relationship between faith and deeds?

_____

_____

_____

_____

_____

7. Do you (and does your church) maintain a good balance between faith and deeds?

_____

_____

_____

_____

_____

8. Using Tom Wright's analogy of the play, what have you learnt over these last three weeks about the script, the characters and the author of the 'biblical play' that helps you continue the play in your own life?

_____

_____

_____

_____

_____

Personal Application

Whilst Acts 2 and 4 gives us a beautiful picture of what
the Early Church looked like immediately after Pentecost,
the rest of the New Testament bears witness to the fact
that it was not always like that! We see people keeping
money for themselves that was meant to help people in
need (Acts 5:1–2); others disregarding the needs of poor
people when taking communion (1 Cor. 11:20–22);
people flashing their wealth through fine clothes and
jewellery (1 Tim. 2:9) and still others judging a person's
value by his or her finances (James 2:1–7). You may feel
that this sounds like a description of some of the faults of
our churches today! It can be easy to point the finger at
others and blame them, but Jesus reminds us always to
look at ourselves first and see where the problems lie
with us (Matt. 7:3–5). Think through what changes need
to happen in your life in order for your church to begin
to look like the picture in Acts 2 and 4.

Seeing Jesus in the Scriptures

Philippians 2:6–11 is a beautiful 'poem' about Jesus. It
speaks of His humility in becoming one of us, a part of
what He had created, and of His willingness to die for us
so that every person might come before God. Paul tells us
that that is what our attitude should be like, too: a
readiness to humble ourselves in order to reach out to
others; to 'consider others better than yourselves' so that
we might 'look not only to [our] own interests, but also to
the interests of others' (vv.3–4).

WEEK 4

The Earth is the Lord's – Caring for God's Earth

Opening Icebreaker

What are your most vivid memories of nature from your childhood?

Bible Readings

- Genesis 1:1–2:3
- Leviticus 25:1–24
- Matthew 6:9–13
- Romans 8:19–21
- Colossians 1:15–20
- Revelation 4

Opening Our Eyes

So far we have looked at our calling to be priests to the people and nations around us, and how a part of that is demonstrating, through the way we live, the character of the God we worship. The foundation for this, on which the rest of the story has been built, has been Genesis 12 and the Exodus event.

However, it will come as no surprise to learn that Genesis 12 isn't actually what the Bible starts with and, in order to get to the real beginning of the story we have been following, we must go back to the creation narrative in Genesis 1 and 2. Here we learn that God created the whole universe and everything in it and declared it to be 'very good' (1:31).

In particular, God created one species to look after everything else that He had made: human beings. The grammar of the Hebrew carries the sense of, 'Let's make humans in our own image, *so that* they may rule over ...'.[1] We see this in the description of humans as made 'in the image of God' (1:26–27). The idea here comes from the nations around Israel in which the king was thought to be the representative of the gods and, in this sense, was described as the god's 'image', representing the presence of the gods in the midst of the people. We, therefore, as the image of God, are to be God's representatives on earth; placed here to 'take care' (2:15) of the rest of creation and enable it to fulfil its purpose of existing for God's glory.

This then is the 'prequel' to what we have seen so far! Yes, our role is to bring others to God, and we do that so individuals can enjoy a relationship with Him, so societies can be transformed and so the whole human race might again pick up its foundational role in looking after the rest of what God has created.

Fundamentally, what today is called 'the environment' matters to God, and it matters to Him how we treat it. There is an inextricable relationship between God, His world and His people throughout the Scriptures. In the Old Testament the land acts as a spiritual barometer of Israel's obedience to Yahweh (eg Deut. 30:15–16; Jer. 5:23–25) and we see how creation delights to praise its Maker (eg Psa. 148; Isa. 55:12). Jesus is linked closely with the earth, so that 'even the winds and the waves obey him' (Mark 4:41) and His death brings forth a huge response from the earth in the form of an earthquake (Matt. 27:51), perhaps echoing the groans of creation in Romans 8:22.[2] It is crucial to understand that God's intention for salvation involves the whole of creation, not just humanity alone. And then when we look to the future (remembering our discussion on Revelation 21 and 22 in Week 2) we see how the rest of creation is involved here, too. Some popular teaching, that the earth will be destroyed when the new age is finally brought in, misses the point. In a manner similar to our own resurrection bodies, there will be both continuity and discontinuity. The emphasis is on transformation rather than destruction.

The responsibility is ours. It is because of us that the rest of creation is in 'bondage to decay' and only when we come back to God and recover our calling will it be set free.

[1] Thanks to Chris Wright for this point.
[2] To look further at Jesus' relationship with the earth, see Bishop James Jones' book, *Jesus and the Earth* (SPCK, 2003).

Discussion Starters

1. What do we learn about God, the land and the people from the commandments of Leviticus 25?

_____

_____

_____

_____

2. Do you think that the land still acts as a spiritual barometer today? Explain your answer.

_____

_____

_____

_____

3. What do you think it means for God's will to be done 'on _earth_ as it is in heaven'?

_____

_____

_____

_____

4. Up until this week, where would you have placed 'the environment' in terms of God's plans for salvation? Use the Romans and Colossians readings to inform your discussion here.

_____

_____

_____

_____

5. How would you answer the charge that our Christian responsibility is to be 'saving souls' and nothing more?

_____

_____

_____

_____

6. In Week 2 we saw how we are to live out our future hope today. How does Revelation 4 add to that understanding?

_____

_____

_____

_____

7. To put it very crudely (there are so many other things we could look at as well), there are four basic areas in our lives in which we can make a difference to God's world:
  • the way we travel

_____

_____

  • the food we eat

_____

_____

  • the energy we use

_____

_____

  • the things we throw away

_____

_____

Look at each of these areas and discuss some practical changes you can make.

Personal Application

It should be fairly obvious that what we have been looking at here applies directly to each one of us! For too long, being concerned for God's earth has been seen as an interest that belongs to pagan and New Age religions and as something that is of only marginal interest to Christians. To be involved in these issues was viewed as somewhat cranky! Thankfully, there have been huge strides taken over recent decades in bringing creation care back into the heart of theology as we have realised the central place that God's world occupies in the biblical story and that it isn't all going to be 'burnt up in the end anyway'. Now the next step is for creation care to come back into the heart of our lives and churches. There is so much we can do here that it is hard to know what to put into this small paragraph![3] We can start to walk or cycle more, buy food produced locally and organically, re-use and recycle as much as we can, and so many other things besides. Whatever we do, we know that we do it in order to be God's representatives on this earth, exercising that authority in a way that reflects His character, not through brutality and carelessness, but with love, compassion and service.

Seeing Jesus in the Scriptures

As images of God, we base our lives on Jesus: 'the image of the invisible God'. He is the One by whom all things were created and He shed his blood so that *all* things might be 'reconciled to him' (Col. 1:15–20).

---

[3] My *L is for Lifestyle: Christian living that doesn't cost the earth* gives lots of tips, as well as more biblical teaching and explanations of the issues facing our planet and its people.

WEEK 5

An Old Problem with a Modern Twist - Trade and Debt

Opening Icebreaker

What did you eat before coming to this meeting? How much do you know of where it came from, how it got to your plate and under what conditions it was produced?

Bible Readings

- Leviticus 25:8–38
- Deuteronomy 15:1–15
- Nehemiah 5:1–13
- Proverbs 13:23
- Amos 8

Opening Our Eyes

The Amos reading talks about a basket of ripe fruit. The fruit in this basket – Israel – is ripe for eating and, having held off for so long, Yahweh has decided that He will wait no longer: 'In that day,' He declares, 'the songs in the temple will turn to wailing. Many, many bodies – flung everywhere! Silence!' (Amos 8:3). What a terrible description of what is going to happen to Israel.

As we saw in the Introduction, Amos is writing during the reign of Jeroboam II (793–753 BC) in a time of peace and prosperity. What a surprise it would be for king and people to hear these words. Hosea spoke of the nation's adultery with other gods and, here, in Amos' words (written at the same time), we see the results of a nation that has turned away from the one God, Yahweh.

In Week 1 we read a passage from Deuteronomy 24, with Israel poised to enter the promised land. As we know, once in the land, Israel eventually chooses the way of disobedience and, as she does so, she rejects Yahweh's commands to be a people demonstrating justice towards one another. The prophets condemn the many ways Israel practises injustice (eg Isa. 10:1–2; Jer. 22:13–17; Ezek. 18:10–13) and the Amos passage is a good description of how the needy and poor are trampled on (8:4) by the way the Israelites act.

These words may have been spoken nearly 3,000 years ago, but they have a familiar ring to them as we look at what is happening in our world today. We see all too often how the rich are able to use the system for their own gain, leading to a situation where, as Proverbs says, 'a poor man's field may produce abundant food, but injustice sweeps it away' (13:23).

Throughout this Bible study we have been seeing how we are to practise justice and compassion towards those who are needy. In Week 2 we looked at the parable of the Good Samaritan and Jesus' command to us to be 'neighbours' and to do as the Samaritan did to the man who had been beaten up. As people who belong to a worldwide Church, and who believe that all people are made in God's image, it is obvious that our 'neighbourliness' extends beyond the person at our front door or in our high street, to people all round the world. If we are to 'spend [ourselves] on behalf of the hungry and satisfy the needs of the oppressed' (Isa. 58:10) then we must learn about, and take action on, the larger issues that cause people to be hungry and oppressed in the first place.

The way our global trading system works and the massive burden of debt that countries have accumulated are two of the main reasons for the increasing inequality that our world is facing. These are complicated issues (see the Leader's Notes) but we cannot stick our heads in the sand, we must try to get to grips with them. Amos is a good example. He was an ordinary person – a shepherd and agricultural worker (7:14). Yet he was courageous enough to be God's mouthpiece. Let us, too, be bold enough to live our lives counterculturally and speak out against the injustices we see.

Discussion Starters

1. Look at the contradiction in Deuteronomy 15:4 and 11. How would you explain that?

_____

_____

_____

_____

2. What are some of the principles that come out from the Deuteronomy 15 reading? Talk about the effects they, and the commands here, would have had on Israelite society, had they been followed.

_____

_____

_____

_____

3. Similarly, what principles come out from the Leviticus 25 reading? What can we learn from them?

_____

_____

_____

_____

4. In what ways is our economy interest-based? What would the effects be of implementing a ban against interest? What benefits would it bring?

_____

_____

_____

_____

5. Nehemiah shows us another situation in which interest is being charged and poor people are being abused. What examples does he give us in the way he acts?

_____

_____

_____

_____

6. Look at Amos 8:4–6. What do you think might be some modern equivalents of what the Israelites were doing?

_____

_____

_____

_____

7. What are the consequences of such injustice (vv.8–14)? Give examples of the way in which we might experience similar consequences today.

_____

_____

_____

_____

8. Dom Helder Camara, a former Brazilian bishop, said, 'When I give food to the poor, they call me a saint. When I ask why the poor have no food, they call me a communist.' Does this quote have relevance to our churches today?

_____

_____

_____

_____

9. How can we start to follow Amos' example in speaking out against the injustices in our world? Do any of you have examples of ways you have already been involved in these issues (eg through Jubilee 2000, now the Jubilee Debt Campaign)?

_____

_____

_____

_____

Personal Application

Unfair trade and the debt problem are issues that we are directly involved with every day of our lives through the things we buy and the banks, investments and pensions that we put our money into. Thus there are everyday things that we can do to take some responsibility in this situation: buying fairly traded goods wherever possible, talking to our banks (etc) about their policies with regards to the debt crisis, trying to move our money to more socially responsible lenders and so on.

These issues, though, are also much bigger than our every-day choices and, like Amos, we can be involved in challenging the big institutions that are involved in perpet-uating the problems. Linking up with the Trade Justice Movement (www.tradejusticemovement.org.uk) and the Jubilee Debt Campaign (www.jubileedebtcampaign.org.uk) is the best way of doing this. Why don't you ask someone from your group to get some information from these organisations to bring to your next meeting and find out some things you could do together?

Seeing Jesus in the Scriptures

In Luke 4, Jesus reflects on the Jubilee when He quotes from Isaiah 61, saying, 'The Spirit of the Lord is on me, because he has anointed me to preach good news to the poor. He has sent me to proclaim freedom for the prisoners and recovery of sight for the blind, to release the oppressed, to proclaim the year of the Lord's favour' (vv.18–19). As He says, 'Today, this scripture is fulfilled in your hearing' (v.21). In Jesus, the year of the Jubilee – the cancellation of debts – has been fulfilled.

WEEK 6

Money – It Makes the World Go Around

Opening Icebreaker

Go on, be honest – what would you do if you won or inherited a large amount of money?!

Bible Readings

- Isaiah 55:1–3
- Matthew 6:24
- Luke 19:1–10
- 2 Corinthians 8:1–13
- Ephesians 4:28

This chapter – and the next – is based on material in J. Odgers, *Simplicity, Love and Justice* (Alpha International, 2004) and R. Valerio, *L is for Lifestyle*.

Opening Our Eyes

Money is our greatest taboo. We don't mind talking about our religious convictions. We might even be honest about our sex lives to a friend. But ask us about our financial affairs and that's a different matter! Our churches often don't help us much either. We probably hear every week that 'God loves a cheerful giver', but does the Bible say anything else about money?[1]

Throughout the Old Testament there appear two strands regarding money and possessions. On the one hand, there is nothing intrinsically wrong with having either and, indeed, some parts of the Old Testament see them as part of the promises of Yahweh for those who live according to His ways (eg Lev. 26:3–5; Deut. 28:1–14). God brings blessing and generosity, rescuing His people *out* of poverty, not calling them into it! Wealth creation is a positive calling that God gives a person and to be denied that ability can be a denial of God's purposes for our lives (eg Joseph in Gen. 39:2–6, and Prov. 3:9–10). We have been placed in a world full of plenty and our response should not be to reject that plenty, but to steward it effectively.

However, wealth is not to be seen necessarily as a reward for covenant faithfulness, and other voices in the Old Testament warn of its dangers (such as with the kings who 'did evil in the eyes of the Lord'). The Old Testament is clear that a person's money or property should never be gained at the expense of another, who is thereby left in a poorer state, and we have seen already the strong denunciations that the prophets make regarding the situation of gross inequality that arose within Israel.

When we turn to look at Jesus we will be disappointed if we hope to find Him only concerned with individual piety! The fact that, to Him, giving is as important as praying and fasting (Matt. 6) and that, apart from the kingdom of God, Jesus talks more about money than about anything else, demonstrates how crucial this issue was to Him. Jesus was very clear that we cannot serve both God and Mammon/Money and taught strongly about the dangers of money. He described riches as a strangler (Luke 8:14) and as a worry (Luke 12:22–34). Money can blind us to the eternal realities of life (Luke 16:19–31) and indeed can be a curse for us (Luke 6:20,24).

More positively, Jesus gives us the flip-side to why we should not be preoccupied with money: because we should *seek first* the kingdom of God (Matt. 6:33). In a wonderful passage, Jesus challenges head-on our society's obsession with material things (our 'treasures') and instead puts before us the values of the kingdom (Matt. 6:19–34).

Money is a complicated issue for us as Christians. It involves all sorts of questions: how much should I give and to what? What about the money I keep? Is it right to invest? If so, in what? What about credit cards and getting into debt? What about pensions and insurance? What is 'ethical investment' and is that something I should aim for? Too many questions to answer in one short session! Through it all, though, let us remember that our aim is to discipline our attitude towards, and our use of, money; to bring it into line with that of the Bible's in order that we might use as much of our money as possible to be a blessing to others.

[1] For a really in-depth look, see C. Blomberg, *Neither Poverty Nor Riches: a biblical theology of money and possessions* (Apollos, 1999).

Discussion Starters

1. A Joseph Rowntree survey found that 95% of those questioned found it offensive to be asked about how they spent their money and whether the choices they were making could be improved upon. Would you put yourself in that 95%?

_____

_____

_____

_____

2. As we have seen, certain passages of the Old Testament teach that material prosperity is a sign of God's blessing (see also Deut. 28:1–14). Do you think this teaching extends into the New Testament?

_____

_____

_____

_____

3. The prophets are clear that a person should not become rich at the expense of someone else, who thereby becomes poorer. Bearing in mind last week's discussions, how does that principle relate to us today?

_____

_____

_____

_____

4. 'You cannot serve both God and Mammon.' In what ways can money become our master today? Give some examples.

_____

_____

_____

_____

5. How do you think we can help each other to serve God and not money?

_____

_____

_____

_____

6. Read through 2 Corinthians 8:1–13. What principles can we learn from that passage about our attitude towards money?

_____

_____

_____

_____

7. The clearest guidance about giving comes in Paul's letters to the Corinthians (1 Cor. 16:1–2; 2 Cor. 8:1–13; 9:6–7). What do they say? How might they apply to your own giving?

_____

_____

_____

_____

8. Do you feel you have a good control on your own financial situation? Do you know exactly how much money you have coming in and how much going out each month?

_____

_____

9. Are there some changes you could make which would release more of your money to help others (or God's world)?

_____

_____

_____

Personal Application

Money is a tricky topic that can leave us feeling defensive, guilty or just downright depressed! However, it needn't lead to any of those feelings and, if handled properly, can instead lead to us being used by God to bless others in a wonderful way. There are three main ways in which we can apply this week's discussions. Firstly, we can look at our attitude: Is money our master? Do we hanker after more of it? Are we able to be content without lots of it? We will look further at these things next week. Secondly, the first step towards getting a handle on our money so we can use it for others is to work out a budget. Edgar Hoover said, 'A budget tells your money where to go, otherwise you wonder where it went'! When we are able to say exactly how much money we have, what we spend, what we save and what we give away, then we can begin to see where there might be areas of weakness that we can work on and where we might have money that we can use to help others. Thirdly, it is a good – if scary! – idea to discuss your finances with another person/couple. They can help you keep on line with any decisions you make and can be there to help you curb your spending, if necessary, or even to encourage you to spend a bit more!

Seeing Jesus in the Scriptures
Read Revelation 3:17–18 and let us remember to focus our lives on what is really important.

WEEK 7

Learning the Art of Contentment

Opening Icebreaker

What object do you value the most and why?

Bible Readings

- Exodus 20:8–11
- Micah 4:1–5
- Matthew 6:19–34
- Philippians 4:11–13
- 1 Timothy 6:6–11

Opening Our Eyes

Romans 12:2 tells us not to 'conform any longer to the pattern of this world', but to 'be transformed by the renewing of your mind'. In order for that to happen we need to understand the forces that are at work causing our minds precisely to be conformed to this world. As we understand them, so we can begin to see how we can counteract them in our lives, that we might be 'living sacrifices' to God, rather than to the gods of our age.

There are many different forces today – we might call them voices – telling us what to believe and how to live. One of the dominant ones is consumerism. At its heart, consumerism is the ultimate pursuit of happiness and fulfilment. This is centred around money as, of course, we need money in order to be able to consume.

As always, we are in a situation far removed from the contexts that the biblical writers spoke or wrote into. They knew nothing of credit cards, advertisements and glossy magazines. And yet, as is clear from the Bible readings, the Bible still has much of relevance to speak into our greedy culture.

In the Old Testament an important law is keeping the Sabbath. This laid important principles regarding rest and trusting God. It speaks to our culture of incessant work, reminding us that our work is not the be-all and end-all and that *we* are not the be-all and end-all. It confirms that, rather than economic achievement, relationship with God, with one another and with our world, is at the heart of what it means to be human and, hence, is our ultimate destiny.

Matthew 6 is, perhaps, the central passage that speaks directly to our situation. Here, the gauntlet is laid down:

what do we put our security in? Is it in God's provision or in our material possessions? Which is more important to us? What are we investing in for the long-term? Do we have an eternal perspective when we consider these things? How important are clothes and food to us? Do we 'run after these things' rather than the kingdom of God?

An overriding biblical theme that is so important for us to recover today is that of contentment. Consumerism makes us think that we need more and more and creates a continual dissatisfaction that is temporarily expunged by a trip to the shops. Its message is that we are not rich enough, beautiful enough, smart enough ... In opposition to these messages, the voices of the Bible tell us to be content: 'Keep your lives free from the love of money and be content with what you have' (Heb. 13:5). Contentment comes from being secure in the knowledge that money and possessions are not the focus of our lives: that honour belongs to Jesus.

One antidote to the seductions of consumerism is the path of simplicity. Simplicity is something that has been embraced by peoples from all faiths and none, but, bearing in mind what we have seen about the Bible's message, it should be something particularly lived out by those who follow Jesus. Jesus said He had come to give us life to the full (John 10:10) and simplicity is about discovering the fullness of life that comes not from having an abundance of money and things, but from having the space for intimacy in our friendships with others and God's wider creation, the space for ourselves and, ultimately, the space for God.

Discussion Starters

1. What principles are enshrined in the Sabbath commandment? How can we live those out today?

_____

_____

_____

_____

2. Dream together about the Micah 4 reading. Imagine a situation such as is envisaged in verse 4. What might it look like today?

_____

_____

_____

_____

3. Read Philippians 4:11–13. Our society tells us that it is our right to be healthy, wealthy and beautiful. What does Jesus promise us?

_____

_____

_____

_____

4. How can we develop contentment in our lives? (As well as the Philippians reading, see also Heb. 13:5 and 1 Tim. 6:6–10.)

_____

_____

_____

_____

5. How do you think consumerism affects our relationships and our commitment to church?

_____

_____

_____

_____

6. The first steps towards simplicity often focus on our use of time, as much as our use of money. Are you happy with your use of time? What values are reflected in what you do? Are there things you could do to use your time better?

_____

_____

_____

_____

7. Have a look at the 'ten steps towards simplicity' in the Personal Application section. Are there any that strike you as particularly interesting or challenging?

_____

_____

_____

_____

Personal Application

Contentment can be an uphill struggle in our society. Simplicity might sound nice, but it is a far from simple option to take. Consider these 'ten steps towards simplicity' from Richard Foster[1]:

- Buy things for their usefulness rather than their status.
- Reject anything that is producing an addiction in you. Learn to distinguish between a real psychological need, like cheerful surroundings, and an addiction.
- Develop the habit of giving things away.
- Refuse to be propagandised by the custodians of modern gadgetry.
- Learn to enjoy things without owning them.
- Develop a deeper appreciation for your creation.
- Look with a healthy scepticism at all 'buy now, pay later' schemes.
- Obey Jesus' instructions about plain, honest speech. 'Let what you say be simply "Yes" or "No"; anything more than this comes from evil' (Matt. 5:37, ESV).
- Reject anything that breeds the oppression of others.
- Shun anything that distracts you from seeking first the kingdom of God.

Think of two changes you can make to your life so that you are moving away from a culture of consumerism and into a culture of contentment.

Seeing Jesus in the Scriptures

Contentment comes from gratitude. 'For you know the grace of our Lord Jesus Christ, that though he was rich, yet for your sakes he became poor, so that you through his poverty might become rich' (2 Cor. 8:9).

Thank You, Jesus, that through You we can discover what it really means to be rich.

[1] Richard Foster, *Freedom of Simplicity* (Triangle, 1995).

Leader's Notes

Week 1: Rivers of Justice in the Old Testament

Opening Icebreaker
As this is the beginning of the study, it is a good idea to
do a very simple icebreaker that will get everyone talking
and will help people begin to get to know one another.
If the group is already well established you can suggest
that the two bits of information that everyone provides
about themselves should be something that no one in the
group would yet know. It can be surprising what new
things you can learn about each other!

Aim of the Session
The aim of this session is quite simple and has already
been made clear in the readings that the group will have
done. It is to help people see how justice is a part of the
foundation of the story of the Old Testament.

There are countless verses that talk of God's concern for
the poor and the marginalised and, therefore, of how
His people also are to look after those who are in need.
Sometimes these verses can be used just like proof texts
– lifted straight out of the Old Testament and applied
directly to our own lives with no attempt at seeing them
in their context. This is often done in an effort to motivate
the Church towards issues of justice. At one level there is
not anything necessarily wrong with this and it can often
be the first step in a person's understanding of these
things. However, when we begin to see how the justice
theme fits in with the broader story of the Old Testament,
that will lead to a fuller appreciation of its fundamental
importance and, from there, to a deeper understanding
of how that theme then continues into our lives. So, make
sure that you yourself are familiar with the basic contours
of the Old Testament story and are clear on Israel's

fundamental calling, and then try always to root what people say in those things.

As you do so, you can then help people apply what they are discussing to their situation today. So, for example, the Isaiah 58 reading is a challenging one for us. Do we fast and long for God to come near us and wonder why He is silent? Maybe we need to learn what it is that God really wants us to do!

One other comment might be helpful to make here. Discussion Starter 1 refers to the relationship between justice and righteousness. This might be a new concept to some people. We mostly know of the idea of righteousness through the New Testament, and Paul in particular, where the emphasis – recovered by the Reformation – is on 'being made right before God', through Jesus. Whilst this emphasis is fundamental, in the Old Testament the idea of righteousness is often accompanied by the idea of justice (eg 1 Kings 10:9; Job 37:23; Psa. 33:5). When we come to the New Testament, the Hebrew word for 'justice' rarely occurs, whereas the word for 'righteousness' occurs often. Because of their inseparably close connection, many New Testament scholars think that the word 'righteousness' in the New Testament (*dikaiosune*) ought to be translated as 'righteousness and justice'. This then gives a new and interesting force to verses such as Matthew 6:33, where we are told therefore to 'seek first his kingdom and his *justice and righteousness*'.

Week 2: Rivers of Justice in Jesus

Opening Icebreaker
This icebreaker is designed to help people get to know one another more. Sometimes we can meet weekly and still not really know what goes on in each other's lives.

This question should give us a bit of an insight and, again, even if we know each other well, we still might learn something new!

Aim of the Session

As will be clear from the Opening Our Eyes section, the focus of this week is on continuing the story that we saw in the Old Testament and seeing how Jesus fits into that as its fulfilment. The aim is to broaden people's understanding as to what Jesus came to this earth to do.

In our Western churches we can sometimes fall into the trap of restricting Jesus' mission too narrowly and concentrating on a purely individual level: ie, 'Jesus came to save me from hell and to give me a relationship with God'. Leaving aside theological debates about the meaning of hell, that sentence is true but, as should be obvious by now, it only goes so far and does not give a full enough representation of God's plans in Jesus. Yes, Jesus died so that we might have a personal relationship with God, but He did that in order that we might then pick up the calling of service given to Israel, to bring other people and nations to God (and the calling extends further than that, too, as we will see in Week 4). As our horizons are widened on this crucial matter, so it becomes clear that we cannot separate out 'spiritual' concerns from those that seem to be more physical or social. Do, therefore, encourage people always to remember this broader understanding of what Jesus came to accomplish.

Turning to some more specific points, Discussion Starter 4 looks at the story of the sheep and the goats in Matthew 25. This is often used as a prime example of how the Bible tells us to get involved with helping the hungry/thirsty and so on. What is generally missed, however, is that the word that Matthew uses in the phrase 'the least of these brothers of mine'/'the least of these' (*elakistos*) is used by Him elsewhere to describe Jesus' disciples. The force of this particular passage, therefore, is not so much on caring for people in general, but on caring for our fellow sisters and brothers in Christ. This ties in with other passages that talk about us loving one another so much that we thereby attract others into our midst (eg John 13:35).

It should be fairly clear by now that I am not advocating a 'Let's look after our own and stuff everyone else' kind of attitude! However, as we look at the Church worldwide, we see terrible inequalities. Some of us enjoy churches with wonderful buildings and technological facilities. We are well fed and comfortable. Other churches struggle with few resources. For their congregations, every day is a fight to find enough food to eat and money to clothe and educate their children. Those of us in the economically wealthier churches have a responsibility to be caring for Christians elsewhere who are hungry, thirsty, naked, or in prison for their faith.

A final comment on Discussion Starter 9: A part of our role as followers of Jesus is to make heaven (by which I don't mean a place, but God's priorities and rule) a reality in our world today, remembering that that will never happen fully until Jesus returns. This has been described as us being 'living parables', living out our future hope in our lives now. This is exciting stuff!

Week 3: Rivers of Justice in the Early Church

Opening Icebreaker
This week's icebreaker can be a good way of finding out a bit of people's 'faith background', as well as being a helpful means of focusing our thoughts on church things.

Aim of the Session
As before, this session continues the story that we started

in Week 1 and so perhaps it would be helpful at this point to give a very brief reminder of that overarching narrative, as it is probably quite a new concept for people. In case *you* need reminding(!), the plot starts with Genesis 12 and Abram's calling to be the founder of the nation of Israel, which is to be a blessing to the other nations. Israel existed to be a priestly nation, standing between the other nations and God. As she failed to do this, a smaller group within Israel (the Levite tribe) was called to be priests, standing between Israel and God, so that Israel might come back to God, so that she might pick up her calling and bring the nations to God. A key part of this was living in a way that demonstrated the character of God as One who loves justice and righteousness.

As God's plans for His creation were continually thwarted by Israel's failure to carry out her calling, Jesus came to bring 'plot resolution'.[1] He was now the ultimate means through whom people could have a relationship with God. The followers of Jesus then become the 'true Israel' who are given Israel's mandate of being a blessing to people throughout the world.

From the example of Jesus and from a fuller under-standing of the Church as the 'true Israel', it should become clear that being concerned for people's physical and social needs is not a sideline concern for a few people in church who think that to be an interesting topic, but is an integral part of our missionary task. It is worth pointing out that the pictures of the Early Church in Acts 2 and 4 are wonderful demonstrations of all aspects of church life working together. Prayer, worship, fellowship, teaching, miracles, communion, looking after

[1] A term taken from J. Middleton and B. Walsh, *Truth is Stranger Than it Used to be: Biblical Faith in a Postmodern Age* (SPCK, 1995. Now publish-ed by IVP), a book to which I am highly indebted for my thinking.

needs, evangelism, seeing growth and so on are all given equal value.

A comment on some of the Discussion Starters might be helpful. Discussion Starter 5 encourages people to start thinking about our churches. It could be easy to get into a 'slanging session' here, so don't forget to remind people of the positive things they said in the Icebreaker! I put this question in because of an example that I came across recently that made me realise how James' instructions are still so relevant to us today. A friend of mine gives lots of money to his church and, a little while ago, the church decided to thank all those who had given money to a particular cause. Those who had given lots were sent a personal letter from the vicar, whilst 'the others' just received a general notice in the church newsletter!

Discussion Starter 8 might lead to some lively discussions. Whilst Tom Wright's analogy is quite widely known, if it is new to people it might cause some consternation, perhaps amongst those who hold a more 'closed' view of the Scriptures. Hopefully, others should find it a particularly refreshing and envisioning approach. If there are people who would like to look at this issue further, point them in the direction of two excellent (and challenging) books: R. Middleton and B. Walsh, *Truth is Stranger Than it Used to be: Biblical Faith in a Postmodern Age* (SPCK, 1995. Now published by IVP), and T. Hart, *Faith Thinking: The Dynamics of Christian Theology* (SPCK, 1995).

Week 4: The Earth is the Lord's – Caring for God's Earth

Opening Icebreaker
Our love for and appreciation of nature was often instilled in us through our experiences as children. Each person in

the group will have some experience to share. It needn't be big and dramatic and city dwellers shouldn't feel inferior to country ramblers! It could be as simple as watching ladybirds in the garden or playing with autumn leaves in the park.

Aim of the Session
In the Introduction to this Bible study guide I explained that we are going to be doing some theological and biblical 'hole filling', particularly in this session. With this in mind, let me here help you to fill in two particular holes.

The first hole is our anthropocentrism. By this I mean the way we separate off humanity from the rest of creation and so think that everything revolves around us and was made for our benefit. Yes, we are the only ones made in God's image, but fundamentally we are a part of the same ecosystems and structures as everything else. When God looks and says 'very good', He does not say that exclusively to humans, but to 'all that he had made' (Gen. 1:31).

This anthropocentrism has coloured how we read the Bible. So, for example, the covenant of Genesis 9 that we say was made with Noah, was actually made with Noah and 'all life on earth' (v.17 and see vv.9–10, 12, 15–17). John 3:16 is another example. When you read that verse, do you implicitly substitute 'the world' for 'people'?! When re-read in the light of the Opening Our Eyes section, we can see that God sent His only Son to die to lead people to eternal life, because of the implications that has for the world that He loves.

The second hole is the one made by the belief that the world is going to be destroyed when Jesus comes again (a point touched on already, but worth looking at further as it is such a big one!). As I said in the Opening Our

Eyes section, the idea of there being a 'new heavens and new earth' (Isa. 65:17; 2 Pet. 3:13; Rev. 21:1) is of transformation rather than destruction. It would be good to let people know that there are two Greek words that we translate 'new': *kainos*, which means 'something that is better than the old' and *neos*, which means 'something that has just appeared for the first time'. The Greek word used in these passages is *kainos*. To give an example, friends of mine have recently had their kitchen re-done. All the old stuff was stripped out and the new flooring and units, and so on, installed. They talked excitedly about their 'new kitchen'! Actually, of course, the original kitchen is still there, but it has now been transformed into something very different to what was there before. It is in this sense that Jesus' return will bring in a new heaven and a new earth.

It is also helpful to think of my friend's kitchen being 'gutted' in relation to 2 Peter 3 and its references to everything being 'reserved for fire' (v.7). Peter's clear message is about judgment: in order for the new to come, the old has to be purged. Verse 10 is variously translated as 'the earth and everything in it will be laid bare/burnt up'. However, both 'laid bare' and 'burnt up' are mistranslations of the Greek: *heurethesetai*, from *heureskein*, 'to find', from which we get the expression, 'Eureka!'. The idea is that, after the purging fire, the earth will be 'found' – a much more positive concept than 'burnt up'!

Week 5: An Old Problem with a Modern Twist – Trade and Debt

Opening Icebreaker
The idea behind this icebreaker is to establish the notion that the way we live our lives – the simple things we do every day without much thought – is connected with

people and land all over the world. Food is often a great starting point to getting people thinking. Learning what lies behind the food we eat opens our eyes to all sorts of issues.

Aim of the Session

As was said in the Opening Our Eyes section, if we want to follow the biblical witness and be a people concerned for seeing God's justice in our world then we need to learn about the contemporary issues we are facing. The aim of this session, therefore, is to learn about the global trading system and the debt crisis and see what responses we can make. With this is mind, the Opening Our Eyes section is designed to look at a biblical perspective to these things and then these Leader's Notes will give you some of the contemporary information that you can teach into the discussion as it arises.

Our global trading system operates under the economic theory of free-trade market capitalism (that is, trade liberalisation, privatisation and financial market deregulation). In other words, the goal that is being worked towards is a world in which nations can trade freely with one another, with no restrictive import tariffs or barriers blocking that trade. Increasing exports to richer countries is a key way in which a poorer country can lift itself out of poverty. The reality though is that the rules for international trade are governed by the commercial and financial interests of those richer countries and so are shaped to their advantage. These rules are shaped primarily through three institutions: the International Monetary Fund, the World Trade Organisation and the World Bank. The result is that since 1981, the poorest countries' share of world trade has fallen by almost a half, to just 0.4%.

The issues are extremely complicated and cannot be dealt with properly in this short section (hence the suggestion for someone to find out more information for next week or, if you are super-prepared, you could do that yourself and bring it to this meeting). Suffice it to say, though, there needs to be a major overhaul of the current system so that the rules work *for* poor people instead of against them.

Many people will know of the debt crisis already through the excellent work of (what was) Jubilee 2000. This is the situation in which banks, rich with money from oil in the 1970s, lent huge sums of money to poorer countries, with low interest. An economic crisis, however, meant that interest rates increased at the same time as the price for basic commodities (the sorts of things the poorer countries were producing: coffee, sugar etc) fell. Countries thus found themselves paying increasing amounts for their debts, whilst receiving less and less from their exports. The result was that the rich countries got more and more money from the poorer countries, which then grew increasingly impoverished. And so we reached the situation where, by 2000, for every £1 given in aid, £13 came back in debt repayments and the basic needs of healthcare and education were sidelined.

Because of Jubilee 2000, much was promised by the rich countries and much was achieved. But there is still a long way to go and many countries still struggle under unsustainable debt, leaving millions of people to suffer. The problem is far from over: there is still much for us to do. Find out more information from the Jubilee Debt Campaign (I have put their web address in the Personal Application section).

Week 6: Money – It Makes the World Go Around

Opening Icebreaker
This is a bit of fun to get people 'warmed up' on the

subject of money. Please make sure you don't get into a discussion about whether or not it's right to 'win' money – that really isn't the point!

Aim of the Session

The aim of this session is to inspire us in our use of money: potentially an exciting thing! For example, I know of one couple with a good income who live very simply. At the end of each financial year they look at what they have earned and what they have spent and they give the surplus away. Last year they gave away £30,000. Of course, not all of us earn a lot of money, but as the story about the widow in Luke 21 shows, quantity is often not the thing that counts.

This session ought to come with a health warning attached – be prepared to tread carefully and handle people's responses wisely. As was said in the Introduction, try to ensure that there is an atmosphere of grace and of openness, encouraging people to lower their defences on this difficult subject. Please be sensitive, too, to the varying financial situations that people are in. You might have some big earners in your group alongside someone struggling on a pension or other state benefits. The majority of your group may well be on a decent income, but still facing a large mortgage and financially-demanding children. This session should not arouse guilt, but should motivate and excite.

There might also be people facing personal debt. A great organisation that can help with this (and many other things such as creating a budget) is Credit Action (www.creditaction.com).

In case you get into some of these discussions, it might be helpful here to say something about savings and investments. Does saving anything demonstrate a lack of faith in God's provision or does *not* saving demonstrate a lack of prudence and good stewardship? The Bible seems to teach both (compare Prov. 6:8 and 21:20 with Matt. 6:19)!

There would seem, biblically, to be two positive grounds given for savings: firstly, in order to fulfil family obligations (Mark 7:9–13; 1 Tim. 5:8) and, secondly, in order not to be dependent on anyone (2 Thess. 3:6–12 and in our society that includes the State). Nowhere does the Bible say we should invest simply to gain more money in order to become more financially secure (compare with Eph. 4:28)!

This still leaves room for interpretation: how far does our family extend? How much should we leave our children? How much do I need to live on to avoid dependence? As so often, the Bible's teaching gives parameters but then does not provide us with a single universally-applicable norm. The appropriate attitude to wealth would seem to depend on the Christian's situation and calling (eg to the mission field, to a dependent family, to singleness etc.).

What we need to remember at all times is our natural inclination to justify saving the most we can! We must always guard ourselves against the desire to accumulate as much as possible in order to make ourselves as secure as possible.

If we do decide to have investments (and remember this extends to having a bank account, mortgage, insurance and pension), we will want that money to be used to benefit God's creation (human and non), rather than harm any aspect of it. To look into 'ethical investments' in more detail, see EIRIS (Ethical Investment Research Service: www.eiris.org).

Week 7: Learning the Art of Contentment

Opening Icebreaker

It can be interesting to hear what things people have that they value the most. It is not necessarily that which is most expensive. Family photos are often what people would most hate to lose in (for example) a house fire.

Aim of the Session

As our concluding week together, this is a chance to focus again on our own lifestyles and how they reflect the values of God's kingdom. So much of what we have looked at in preceding weeks hinges on how we outwork it in our lives: we can have perfect theology, but that means nothing if we don't live that theology out in practice.

The affluent lifestyles and over-consumption of economically-developed countries lies behind a lot of what we have seen already, and so it is good to focus in on consumerism and begin to discuss how we can tackle it. In these Leader's Notes it will be helpful to give a further description of what consumerism is, which you can then feed back into the group discussion.

At its most basic, consumerism is the culture whereby our primary activity and focus is on consuming things, rather than producing them. There need not necessarily be anything wrong in this. We have been made to consume and, with a positive view of creation, our consumption of goods can be a blessing that allows our needs to be met. However, the danger is that, as we consume, so we allow ourselves to be consumed by the ideology of consumerism that overtakes us.

The result is that consumerism has now become the dominant force in our society and, as such, carries with it some very powerful values. A person's identity and significance is defined by what he or she consumes, whether that be his or her house, car, holiday, hair product, clothes or whatever. Goods are valued for what they mean as much as for their use.

In the past, people's identity was bound up with their family, their faith, their values and their location. Now, identity is primarily found in what we consume and often people will build their supporting community around their consumption habits. Think of your family and friends and ask yourself to what extent your bonding with them is done around the things you consume (eg dinner out, a shopping trip)? How much of your conversation is about activities or objects of consumption (thanks to Tom and Christine Sine for this point)?

The consumer culture that most of us reading this will live in is profoundly individualistic and self-centred. It stresses the autonomy of individuals and individuals' rights to have whatever they want and to be whomever they want – all at the cheapest price they can get.

The global picture of consumerism is of a world struggling to meet the demand for more, more, more. There are many causes of poverty: sinful personal choices, disasters, lack of technology, Western colonialism, corruption and so on, but we have to recognise that our consumerism is a part of the unjust structures that contribute to world poverty.

The positive side is that we do have a choice as to how we live our lives and how we spend our money. As we have seen in earlier weeks, we do have the power to consume in a way that actually helps alleviate poverty. However, it's not just about consuming in a way that appeases our conscience and allows us to keep buying lots of things! This week's session should challenge us to reconsider not only *how* we consume but also *how much* we consume.

National Distributors

UK: (and countries not listed below)
CWR, Waverley Abbey House, Waverley Lane, Farnham, Surrey GU9 8EP.
Tel: (01252) 784700 Outside UK +44 1252 784700

AUSTRALIA: CMC Australasia, PO Box 519, Belmont, Victoria 3216.
Tel: (03) 5241 3288

CANADA: Cook Communications Ministries, PO Box 98, 55 Woodslee Avenue, Paris, Ontario.
Tel: 1800 263 2664

GHANA: Challenge Enterprises of Ghana, PO Box 5723, Accra.
Tel: (021) 222437/223249 Fax: (021) 226227

HONG KONG: Cross Communications Ltd, 1/F, 562A Nathan Road, Kowloon.
Tel: 2780 1188 Fax: 2770 6229

INDIA: Crystal Communications, 10-3-18/4/1, East Marredpalli, Secunderabad – 500026,
Andhra Pradesh.
Tel/Fax: (040) 27737145

KENYA: Keswick Books and Gifts Ltd, PO Box 10242, Nairobi.
Tel: (02) 331692/226047 Fax: (02) 728557

MALAYSIA: Salvation Book Centre (M) Sdn Bhd, 23 Jalan SS 2/64, 47300 Petaling Jaya, Selangor.
Tel: (03) 78766411/78766797 Fax: (03) 78757066/78756360

NEW ZEALAND: CMC Australasia, PO Box 36015, Lower Hutt.
Tel: 0800 449 408 Fax: 0800 449 049

NIGERIA: FBFM, Helen Baugh House, 96 St Finbarr's College Road, Akoka, Lagos.
Tel: (01) 7747429/4700218/825775/827264

PHILIPPINES: OMF Literature Inc, 776 Boni Avenue, Mandaluyong City.
Tel: (02) 531 2183 Fax: (02) 531 1960

SINGAPORE: Armour Publishing Pte Ltd, Block 203A Henderson Road,
11–06 Henderson Industrial Park, Singapore 159546.
Tel: 6 276 9976 Fax: 6 276 7564

SOUTH AFRICA: Struik Christian Books, 80 MacKenzie Street, PO Box 1144, Cape Town 8000.
Tel: (021) 462 4360 Fax: (021) 461 3612

SRI LANKA: Christombu Books, 27 Hospital Street, Colombo 1.
Tel: (01) 433142/328909

TANZANIA: CLC Christian Book Centre, PO Box 1384, Mkwepu Street, Dar es Salaam.
Tel/Fax: (022) 2119439

USA: Cook Communications Ministries, PO Box 98, 55 Woodslee Avenue, Paris, Ontario, Canada.
Tel: 1800 263 2664

ZIMBABWE: Word of Life Books, Shop 4, Memorial Building, 35 S Machel Avenue, Harare.
Tel: (04) 781305 Fax: (04) 774739

For email addresses, visit the CWR website: www.cwr.org.uk
CWR is a registered charity - number 294387

Day and Residential Courses

Counselling Training

Leadership Development

Biblical Study Courses

Regional Seminars

Ministry to Women

Daily Devotionals

Books and Videos

Conference Centre

Trusted all Over the World

CWR HAS GAINED A WORLDWIDE reputation as a centre of excellence for Bible-based training and resources. From our headquarters at Waverley Abbey House, Farnham, England, we have been serving God's people for 40 years with a vision to help apply God's Word to everyday life and relationships. The daily devotional *Every Day with Jesus* is read by over three-quarters of a million people in more than 150 countries, and our unique courses in biblical studies and pastoral care are respected all over the world. Waverley Abbey House provides a conference centre in a tranquil setting.

For free brochures on our seminars and courses, conference facilities, or a catalogue of CWR resources, please contact us at the following address. **CWR, Waverley Abbey House, Waverley Lane, Farnham, Surrey GU9 8EP, UK**

Telephone: +44 (0)1252 784700
Email: mail@cwr.org.uk
Website: www.cwr.org.uk

CWR CRUSADE FOR WORLD REVIVAL
Applying God's Word to everyday life and relationships

New titles in the fast-growing *Cover to Cover* series

Moses
Face to face with God
Elizabeth Rundle
ISBN: 1-85345-336-6

2 Timothy and Titus
Vital Christianity
Christine Platt
ISBN: 1-85345-338-2

Rivers of Justice
Responding to God's call to righteousness today
Ruth Valerio
ISBN: 1-85345-339-0

Nehemiah
Principles for life
Selwyn Hughes with Ian Sewter
ISBN: 1-85345-335-8

Hebrews
Jesus – simply the best
John Houghton
ISBN: 1-85345-337-4

Parables
Communicating God on earth
Chris Leonard
ISBN: 1-85345-340-4

£3.99 each (plus p&p)

Other titles in this series

Hosea
The love that never fails
*Selwyn Hughes
with Ian Sewter*
ISBN: 1-85345-290-4

James
Faith in action
Trevor J. Partridge
ISBN: 1-85345-293-9

God's Rescue Plan
Finding God's
fingerprints on human
history
Catherine Butcher
ISBN: 1-85345-294-7

1 Timothy
Healthy churches –
effective Christians
Chrisine Platt
ISBN: 1-85345-291-2

The Divine Blueprint
God's extraordinary
power in ordinary lives
Gary Pritchard
ISBN: 1-85345-292-0

John's Gospel
Exploring the seven
miraculous signs
Keith Hacking
ISBN: 1-85345-295-5

The Kingdom
Studies from Matthew's
Gospel
Chris Leonard
ISBN: 1-85345-251-3

**The Letter to the
Romans**
Good news for
everyone
John Houghton
ISBN: 1-85345-250-5

The Covenants
God's promise and their
relevance today
John Houghton
ISBN: 1-85345-255-6

Joseph
The power of
forgiveness and
reconciliation
Elizabeth Rundle
ISBN: 1-85345-252-1

**Great Prayers
of the Bible**
Applying them to
our lives today
Jennifer Oldroyd
ISBN: 1-85345-253-X

The Holy Spirit
Understanding and
experiencing Him
*Selwyn Hughes
with Ian Sewter*
ISBN: 1-85345-254-8

The Image of God
His attributes and
character
Trevor J. Partridge
ISBN: 1-85345-228-9

The Tabernacle
Entering God's
presence
Ian Sewter
ISBN: 1-85345-230-0

**The Uniqueness of
our Faith**
What makes Christianity
distinctive?
*Selwyn Hughes
with Ian Sewter*
ISBN: 1-85345-232-7

Ruth
Loving Kindness
in Action
Elizabeth Rundle
ISBN: 1-85345-231-9

Mark
Life as it is meant
to be lived
Christine Platt
ISBN: 1-85345-233-5

Ephesians
Claiming your
inheritance
Trevor J. Partridge
ISBN: 1-85345-229-7

£3.99 each (plus p&p)